The
Feeling
May
Remain

The Feeling May Remain

Akif Kichloo

First edition published globally by
Read Out Loud Publishing LLP in 2016.

ISBN: 978-81-931360-7-2

Cover photograph and design by Adnan Khateeb & Akif Kichloo
www.akifkichloobooks.com

Interior designed by E.M Tippetts Book Designs.
www.emtippettsbookdesigns.com

The feeling may remain,
but
the healing must continue…

Table of Contents

For

Dad and my sweet munchkin nephew, Adam

In this we live,
In this we love,
In this we die.

What Starves You Carves You

That's the thing about love they don't understand:

It shapes you in its absence too.

Seasons

I fell in love with the spring in you;
the blossoming forsythias and the lilacs in bloom.
Silk scarves, satin sheets, and us blazing through that
season in the safety of our cocoon.

Then the warm summer breeze blew us away.
The pale autumn moon growing smaller by the day, and
at the end of it, the moon completely disappeared,
and we were neck deep in each other's mess;
the forsythias shriveled and the lilacs dead—
crushed under our harsh snow boots and regret.

Now we live two completely different lives.
Waiting eagerly for more springs to come,

more summers to stay,
and at the same time dreading those winters,
for now we know, when it gets colder—
people often say their good-byes and leave.

Winter Is Late

Winter is late this year;

its return postponed,

for the gods above the clouds know

my fear of cold shoulders.

I have been running from the snow

for as long as I can remember,

and now that I have gathered

enough conviction,

the snow seems to be

running from me.

Give me cold hands

and I will warm them this instant.

Give me extinguished fires and I will

reignite the flames in a fraction of bits.

It's the foggy eyes I know not what to do with.

It's the sooted hearts I know not how to clean.

Declaration

I love you. Not the concept of you. Not the perception of you. Not what you will become. Not your prospects. Not your need to be loved. I love you. Today. Right now. Just as you are. And I know, with time we will change. We will evolve. We will grow. And I hope we do all of it together. But I don't ask anything from you other than what we have now. I don't expect you to promise me anything in return. Because I love you for you, and the promises you are unable to make today don't change anything.

What Now?

What about your dreams that

lie forgotten in my eyes?

What about the promise of your

heart entangled with mine?

We will always be this.

We will always be that—

Like tiny grains of wheat,

minuscule—

now we lie scattered in barns no one visits

anymore.

Who shall see us now?

Who shall find us worthy enough to eat?

Realization

We are all looking for
something we already
have, when all we need
is the realization that
we are complete.

Those Fights

Where do you keep me if you don't keep me in your memories anymore? Did I just disappear overnight like a bad dream, or did I fade with time like those childhood memories you cannot remember anymore? Did I haunt you for a while when you tried to press on with your life, or did I come in the way of what you had to accomplish? Was I the push you needed or the stop that annoyed you day in and day out?

Did you finally manage to fall in love with the rain? What about my photograph you kept hidden in the back of your wallet? Did it age with grace, or did it wrinkle and fade the way we did?

Did you give up those smokes you needed so bad every time we fought, or do you not need them anymore? Does he not fight with you like I did? Do you miss those fights? Has peace been kind to you the way it has been cruel to me? What would you choose if you had to choose today? Wait, don't answer that.

I miss those fights.

About You

"Dig deep," they say, "to find the emotion inside."

Little do they know, you live on my fingertips.

The Problem

Sometimes we are

more doubt than trust,

more talk than touch,

more tomorrow than today,

and worst of all—

more who we let go than

who we let stay.

That's the problem.

Lullaby

Some days I don't know anything and still in everything you belong. You are hard to remember and at the same time impossible to forget.

(So it hurts when I come to mind?)

Immensely, but it also puts me to sleep every night.

Everything

How is it that I am both the animal caught

in the headlights, frozen in shock,

and also the speeding car, the vivacious

death heading toward me?

How am I all the names you call

me in secret, behind my back,

and also the love you carry hidden in the

curvature of your back, the strength

in your spine?

How am I both the wishbone as well as the bet;

The sour delicacy, the sweet surrender—both

the promise and the regret?

I think I have been here for centuries, having

lived many lives,

How otherwise am I both the thousand

shattered pieces of glass glittering on the floor

and also those thousand different reflections you
see in them?
How otherwise am I both the deer wandering
this earth and also the musk it was killed for?

Weekend

Never have I loved this creaky

floor more than now when you walk on it,

fresh out of a shower, eyeing me from across the room,

hair dripping wet, half gold, half fruit,

and tapioca, truffle, and chocolate whiff hugging the

disheveled sheets from all that was ravished—skin for

plates,

lips for hands, and appetites as big as

the moment itself.

Even sleep won't feel shy tonight,

and the morning alarm—just a bell for round two.

Pyramids

I build pyramids of passion
and lay them on you
like castles made of matchsticks.
And day after day,
you make sure
that the fire in your heart
doesn't burn these castles
away.

You break down complexities
into something as simple
as a good-morning
kiss.
And I am simply learning
from you,

that it is not the fire in
us that burns all we have,
but the fire in us that
we let slip away.

I Love You

There is no surprise, reason,

logic, or abomination

in this sentence

when I declare my love for you.

All I know is that you belong to me,

I belong to you,

and this world belongs to us.

There is no division between the good

and the bad in my love for you.

No wall between the perks of having you to love

and the agony of love itself.

The only reason I love you

is because I love you.

There is nothing else.

And if there is god,

if there are a hundred gods,

and I am given a choice,

I would rather have you.

They can keep the rest.

Burnt

People judge a book by its cover
and if this is to be believed, then she is carefree,
the most jovial of us all.

But if you look with a caring eye,
behind her smile,
you can see the worn-out pavements of her mind
and tar-coated chimney walls of her heart,
from years of juggling with fire.

The kind of fire that holds no promise but one:
The promise to burn.

Awareness Is the Key

Let us ignore the stars tonight

and gaze at the immense nothingness in between,

for what sparkles is always the center of

attention of the world

and what doesn't—often sits quiet and alone.

And quiet will always tell you more.

Just like lonely will always love you more.

Her Gentle Request

She said,

Love me slowly,
wildly, but tenderly.

Kiss me like the grain of dust kissing your favorite book,
sitting unread and lonely on your desk for days.
Touch me like the rays of sun touch your skin
through the windowpane
at the commencement of a warm summer day.

Love me slowly,
madly, but gently.

Rub my skin and feel the warmth it holds from within,
and see that no sun can hold this warmth for you.
Brush my hips and measure the insecurities I've tackled
in every home I made
with every inch of these imperfect bones.

Graze my legs and follow the trail of every road I've traced
to the graveyards of surrender and grace.

Watch me speak, lover,
and let the rain of your love wash the dirt
of endless apologies away from my tongue.
Look through me now, and see the ache brimming
in every sentence I make in my head but stutter to give
away.

There is not one speckle of regret in my bones.
Not one glint of guilt in my being.
I have turned sorrow into grace,
disappointment into courage;

every freckle on my skin is a fucking black hole
where time froze to keep all my memories safe.

These long arms are meant to be put around one worthy
of love.
These comely knees are meant to be claimed by
one worthy of passion.

These weary feet are meant to walk into your door, love,
locking the shame of yesteryears away.

So
When you do,

Love me slowly
Love me kindly
Love me wildly...

In Totality

There are people living inside of me. Some loving, some angry, some quiet, some bitter, some wise, and some with no voice. It is a struggle. It is a constant battle. Every moment a different person wins, and that moment belongs to them. I am so many people that sometimes I become them all. And at those times I am closest to my name. At those times I am not a fragment anymore, but a being. Hopefully one that can love not in pieces but wholly. Like beings are supposed to love and be loved. In totality.

Treat Yourself with Kindness

You lift your hands in disbelief, raise your voice with contempt, every time someone speaks low of you. And yet every morning you stand in front of that mirror and say things like "I wish I was thinner. I wish I looked more like that person who is idolized." And you think this is fine. You think this is normal. You have never once cut yourself or even thought of any form of self-harm, yet unknowingly you have been abusing yourself for so long with these ridiculous statements of derision and disregard. So long that you don't even notice it anymore. As if it is okay for you to call yourself names. As if you are less of a person than anybody else.

Please treat yourself with kindness.

Take Charge

Healing yourself is

your own responsibility.

Tearing you apart was theirs.

And they did a hell of a job.

Tough to Find

"I don't care much. About what people think. What people say. All that keeps changing. What matters is love. And what you make out of yourself. And what you make out of people when you are around them. I think I have said too much. I must stop now."

"You shouldn't."

"Don't be so reckless with me."

"Why not?"

"'Cause I am a person. And a good one. We are tough to find."

Where I Belong

Can the weight of your lips

now rest against my skin,

the scent of your incense

lean against my fingertips?

I am all words and no meaning

without your presence,

all stories and no laughter

without your touch.

I have a longing for your kiss

and a belonging to your skin;

if I don't inhabit you now,

I will perish. I will wither.

Hands

Hands have a way of doing and undoing;
a manner of telling us progressions
our mind's not aware of yet.

They reach out and touch things.
Feel them even with eyes closed.

Often they reach out and hold another's hand,
and it feels right.
Like their knuckles were the last few pieces
of the jigsaw puzzle
our hands had been stuck without for years.

Hands always fall in love first.
Long before your heart gets the clue.
And often they find you that one thing
you have been looking for all your life.

Believe your hands.

Butterflies in Early Spring

An unburdened smile rising with the sun;

your face is all the answers as one.

Something means more than what I see,

tastes a little different with every kiss,

and I am not eager to know all the flavors so fast.

Minute to minute, hour to hour, season to season

I'll hold your bits and save them in my precious jars;

like children collecting butterflies in early spring.

Midnight Rain

From across the room your gaze caught mine, and I saw how your eyes lit up the very second they mirrored my face. I felt the spark too, which soon turned into a forest fire, and then you looked away.

I couldn't find the courage to walk up to you, and I think you were too proud to do the same.

It was almost midnight then, and the room was filled with tipsy souls swaying with the sound of rain that cleansed all those beats that lousy DJ played, and all I could think in that moment was whether you could feel my burning flesh as we danced outside, in the open, under the pouring rain.

"It takes more than one night of downpour to control fires like these," I still remember you had said the next day.

"I hope it takes us a lifetime," I had quietly exclaimed.

Wishing Wells

Let us jump into those wishing wells tonight

and take all our pennies back.

Let us watch a shooting star tonight

and not make a wish.

Let us be here now.

Holding hands.

Watching this shimmery sky turn into the

beginning of a new day — the most beautiful of days.

And let us hope we understand now,

that all we wished for and never got in life,

led us to this—

You. I. And these endless stars of the night

blinking at us in the most humble of ways.

Home

People keep asking
me for my address and
I keep handing them
your name.

Epiphany

Sometimes the most beautiful of flowers die.

This never means that another such will never be born

again.

Patience, virtue, and faith;

the whole universe is yours

only if you have the patience to wait for the next,

the virtue to accept that it is yours to keep,

and the faith to believe that once it arrives, it is here to

stay.

Like Always

The calendar turns not on your skin,

the seasons too never change.

Even when the world is chilly

and the insides of your bones ache,

I find warmth near you—tonight, like always.

Change

"Never change," she said, gripping my arm
tight, as if I were the summer and she knew autumn
was nearing.

Perfect Teacher

I never knew we could challenge the inevitable. Never understood what was bound to happen could be stopped. Then I saw her struggle. Fighting every day and everything; patiently, quietly, and oftentimes hands on. Her perseverance changed me. Turned some stones inside my soul. Now I know *carefree* is as much a struggle as *careful*. You have got to learn to fight the odds. And I must say, she did quite a job.

Yes, she was the perfect teacher. Women generally are, if only men could find a way to pay more attention to their actions and less to their needs, a little less to their breasts and more to their feet. But it's ego that makes us men such bad students. We assume women need us more if not as much as we need them. What fools!

Prayer for Women I Know

May you be granted the experience of a hurricane,
for the wind of chaos blows through your life like a
breeze.

May the ferocity of thunder be granted to your voice, so
their rain like noise falls silent when
you speak.

May you be the leader,
and your caravan comprise men of principle
and not just men of fate.

The rise and fall of nations depends on your smile.
May you be granted wisdom to understand that you are
precious,
for men without you are forever tyrants, butchers,
and hungry flycatchers.

Self-Doubt I

Why are you wasting your years
trying to question what you deserve?

Let me tell you one thing and one thing only:

You deserve a love so surreal that it
feels philosophical.

Self-Doubt II

Who planted this seed of self-doubt in your heart?
Was it the vampire men who only came to you at dusk
and disappeared like magic in the morning light,
or the bastard bums who came looking for you
so they could quench their thirst
sucking on whiskey neat in your blood
leaving the very moment there was none left to feed
their lust?

Did they bring seeds with them and promise you
gardens,
and did you try to find sweet in the bitter tangerines
they ended up handing you,
and did your heart break when they blamed you for the
bad taste?

What image did your father leave for you of other men?
Was he the example you would have wanted him to set,
or was he unkind to your mother like the rest of them?

If he was the perfect man like you say,

did he warn you to refrain from renting your heart out?

And if he did,

did he also mention that if you absolutely have to do it,

if you feel no other choice in your heart than to do it,

at least do not rent it to cowards?

I hope he did,

because men who are cowards have no place in the

sanctum of your heart.

Not even for a short stay.

Heaven

The sound of silence

And the noise of our kiss;

That's my heaven.

Your Secrets

Tell me what you're saying in your heart when you stay
absolutely silent?
Which song plays in your head when you cry?

Tell me about the time when you felt hate more
than you felt love.
An instance when you had to resort to violence?
Tell me about the boy who broke your heart.

Share with me, a memory you resent the most.
Say your favorite curse word.
Show the part of your body that you 'kind of hate'.

I want to know every side of you;
Even the sides you are not proud of—need to be loved.

Bliss

I crash into you more

each time I try to

escape you.

I don't know the

beginnings

of you,

but

I know for sure

that I don't

want to see

where you

end.

Bury Your Needs in Me

I know there are times when you just want to lose your mind and let the madness treat you to something more. Something that sanity knows not of. I want you to know that it is okay if you do. And if you don't believe me, still, let me lose my mind with you.

I see burning castles surround every realm of your world, and I know you are scared. But hand over the weapons now, lover. Get rid of the gasoline you keep ready inside your chest. I am here now, and I am not here to wage wars so you change your life. That is not my style. I am here to burn with you.

Ordinary

Mesmerized by the eyes of your heart

That you see me for who I am—

when all I am is tired,

from all the onlookers watching me

for what I might become;

I am nothing but ordinary

and you see me as such,

And this, my love, has made

all the difference in the world.

Monsters

We cannot run from ourselves. We can only protect ourselves from turning into people we swore we would never become.

New Beginnings

We don't drink from the bottles

that emptied us anymore;

Now we fill each other's void.

Some Days

Some days you find yourself at the crossroads
Where everywhere you look, you see the end looking
back at you.
Some days the only meaning of triumph you know
is you driving into a tree trunk and successfully killing
yourself.

The toothbrush feels like razor blades,
scraping the last of happy from your gums,
and your sink stinks of blood,
filled with memories that lasted decades,
of the times that didn't.

Some days their boomerang tongues orbit your ears like
planets slaving around the sun,
and you hope for tsunamis,
you wish for floods to come and drown you,
for the air in your lungs aches so much,
and breathing is too much work.

The night-blooming jasmine on your balcony refuses to
open up,
and the Los Angeles night feels like death knell.

Some days you don't feel okay.
And I want you to know
that it's okay to feel that way.
We all have been there
and we all have lived through it.
We all break, and then we heal.
You will too. You are not alone in this.

Snow Flakes

In the scheme of all things big,

we are but snowflakes

dancing delightfully midair,

destined to land graciously

on silent grounds atop mountains.

If only we knew

snowflakes feel no shame as they fall.

They don't tumble, they don't flutter,

but descend with such grace.

And when they are touched,

they don't hold their cold inside.

Instead, they melt and give it up;

they give all their rigor away.

Memory

If I am nothing but a memory,

let me reside in you,

beside the sad ones, the old ones,

and the ones you don't have to remember exist.

Let me be the one of many things you know,

but don't know that you do,

until the time comes right and you need them,

so you collect them,

and they come together as florets of dandelions

to form the most beautiful weed there is.

Let me be in you.

Let me be forgotten somewhere in the holts

of your head.

White Light

I promise to be your white light

when the world sees you through a prism of judgment

and splits you into statements, tags, and petty names.

You are more than that.

You are not just a metaphor to be used in a poem

but the reason for men of this world to wake up

every morning and dream.

Writing

She lives in my words,

breathes in the spaces in between.

And with every punctuation mark

she holds her breath a little

If I stop writing—

she ceases to exist.

Wallflower

There is nothing sexier than watching a wallflower like you bloom into the most sultry mistress in the dead of night.

Do me, you say.

What is it that I should do?
Should I gently make love to the tender body of that shy introvert you are at 2:00 p.m., or should I rampage the wild
beast you become at 2:00 a.m.?

Tell me?

2:00 a.m.

I love you more at 2:00 a.m.
This doesn't mean I love you less
any other time.

Be Warm

Late at night,

some part of the world often forgets

that there is sun shining abundantly still,

on some faraway land,

until it's morning again

and again there is light.

Be that light.

Be the morning when there seems no sun.

There are always people working late-night shifts,

and when they come home

the worries of the next day keep their sleep at bay.

Be the calm when they are done.

Be the triumph in that one last thing

before someone decides to give up and run.

Be the stillness in the mind of a drunk.

Be that beautiful thought

that stops a girl holding a scalpel to her wrist

because she was told she looked

ugly in her prom dress.

Be the kindness that stops a bully.

Be the balm to the bruises of ones who hurt the most.

Be warm!

When the world is cold to you,

That's the perfect time to cozy it.

Shower it with your warmth.

And please, for god's sake, don't expect rewards in

return.

Old Lovers

It's late

and I hear crickets chirp on one side

and clouds growl on the other.

Don't know who they call out like this so late at night.

They must be young, I think to myself,

and oh so innocent.

With time, like me,

they too will learn to remember old lovers in silence.

Courage

Rest now the fight

to question the intent

of others.

Come now the courage

to accept them with their

faults.

Hope in My Sorrow

There is hope in my sorrow; a distant creak of a familiar sound that keeps me walking, in search of the source of its coming, and more so in hopes of finding you.
You have lost yourself to find yourself.

There is hope in my sorrow; a dreaded wish, a chameleon sighting—color blind to omnipresent black.
Invisibility doesn't hide you. The lack of loving does.

There is hope in my sorrow; a glimpse of red—spilled wine and lips touching rims of glasses to draw maps that lead me to you.
Home is sometimes a person too.

There is hope in my sorrow, and so is utmost madness.
I find you every day, and then I wake up.

Too Many Sides

She wears truth like a crown

Yet no ring on her digits

Her eyes reflect the smile

That she wears on her lips

I never ask her of her past

Yet I wonder what she hides

Under that soft skin and thick mascara;

This girl with one too many sides.

Let Go

In gusts of rain
The dead leaves sink;
Rain puddles—autumn
graves of nature.

One leaf still clings
To a tree where it lived,
But change is one
riveting teacher.

Lesson it brings
As the storm comes in,
With the force of a
thousand glaciers.

Letting go of the tree,
The leaf swirls to the ground,
Conceding to rules
of the Maker.

Free it falls

And free it feels;

Triumphant, what

it'd deemed failure.

At times cruel

But if we let go,

Change will always

be our savior.

Kiss

She loved me long before I knew a kiss.

She kissed me long before I knew a kiss meant

something.

She left icicles on my lips when she left,

and that cold still cradles me when I embrace someone

new;

Always reminding me

that it's not just the act of passion when we kiss

someone,

but an act of promising someone our heart.

Your Touch

I have been sleeping with the ghost of you;

chasing a dragon for years.

Every morning when I wake up,

I wake up with a smile,

which soon empties itself

like the empty side of my bed.

I have wanted you, my love,

as much in daylight

as I have craved you in the dead of night.

I have lost you

and again dreamt you back into this life.

I have forgotten your voice,

but I hear you, still.

I am happy, dear love, without you,

but I am forever hungry for your touch.

Good-bye Poems

I have written you so many good-bye poems
that these hands look like daisies planted near your
tomb,
and I am still writing,
and often when I think about you, I write of love.

Not the kind that slips through your fingers
and disappears into the sea, but the kind that stays.

You see, they were right when they said,
you crave what you don't have,
and when you have it,
there is no way you can value it for too long.

Love oftentimes is overrated,
and yes, why not, I am still paying its price—
in installments, with EMI rates so high
that your banks have stopped asking me for more.
Even they know I have nothing to give,

but, love, love keeps knocking at my door
and I don't know what to do with it.

So, I write obituaries, quoting dead poets who are not
here,
like you are not here.
You see, they were right when they said,
you crave what you don't have,
and when you have it, there is no way you can value it
for long.

And, love, your bills still keep piling in my chest,
even when my address is not your home anymore.

(Maybe) your tombstone has these inscribed now;
all these poems I keep writing to you,
and I don't know if you know it,
but last night it exploded in my chest,
and god is my witness,
there was not one poem of regret near your grave;
only kindhearted good-byes and daisies.

Fondness or Regret

I recall your eyes, for the rest has faded with time. What do you remember of me?

(Your voice.)

Which one? The one filled with promises of a forever or the shrilled, unsure one at the end?

(How does it matter?)

It matters to me. I want to know if you remember me with fondness or regret.

Your Thoughts

You are on my mind tonight.

I close my eyes and I see you.

I open them and you disappear,

and just like that my wounds come unstitched,

my heart starts to beat your heartbeat,

and that is the only sound I want to hear.

Do you feel it too, lover?

Do you know when I think of you?

Does it get in your way when I miss you like I miss you

today?

Do you feel not home even when you are in your home

like I do when you are not with me?

I have a hundred chores to take care of,

but my eyes find that one thing that reminds me of you,

and my frosty mind thaws with your thoughts,

and the icicles on my lips start to drip wonder.

You know there are snowy flowers

growing on the windowpanes of my soul;

hence the light doesn't get in as much.

How do you still get in with such ease, lover?

How is my mind still filled with so many icy flowers of

you,

waiting to melt with the sweet embrace of your thought?

Different

People leave everything rattled when they go,

but this one was different.

She brought devastation with her;

the kind you know many stars must have died to create.

Every time she arrived,

I felt earthquakes dismantle everything in my chest

and volcanoes erupt on my neck like gasoline to a flame.

The silence was always deafening when she left.

When everyone worshipped the moon,

this one talked of the sun

She made love like thunderstorms

and it rained fire every time she kissed.

She was the kind of girl even meth-heads would run
from

if they knew what she was made of.

She was the supreme addiction; the fatal kind.

Personal Revolution

They came and they left.

You cried, but you stood your ground.

You stayed tethered to hope as well as

committed to dignified dreams

and little victories of day-to-day life.

You felt different.

Then you started to change.

Your smile returned with reticence

before completely taking over your face.

Today, you are no longer afraid to let that smile be there,

and now you understand it was not about them.

It was never about anyone else.

This was about you from the day you were born.

This was about you learning to love yourself—

not letting the inferiority of the external corrupt

the piety of the internal.

This was your personal revolution.

This was the uprising of your lifetime.

And you won.

Do You Know?

One day I might find you and want to touch you.
What if I see you and want to kiss you?

It has been years I have been following a silhouette I
think is you, and it has been years I have tried to catch it.
They always told me
love would be a light that would come chasing me,
but the shadow looks more you than any light I see.

Do you see me too?
And do you know that we are going to meet one day?

Some Are Born Lovers

Lovers without lovers often feel homesick,

until they fall in love with their loneliness.

Broken Heart

"How do you mend a broken heart?"

"You don't mend a broken heart.
You distract it."

The Words

And then when our mouths were shut

and not a word could find its way out of our tongues,

didn't our hands do the talking for us,

moving up and then down

and then right and left

and everywhere,

telling us all the things we needed to know.

Wasn't it love when I touched you,

and wasn't it love when you lay next to me

spewing looks instead of words,

and didn't I understand?

Words only mean something if you speak them,

and my skin spoke more than the muscles in my tongue

could,

and didn't my eyes beg you to stay,

didn't my legs freeze and my knees bend,

shattering into the ground,

and didn't my shoulders droop,

breaking my back into a hump

and didn't I close my eyes so as not to

watch you walk away?

What if my lips didn't move,

what if air refused to form syllables on my gums?

I spoke my mind out when I first met you,

and I spoke my mind out the day you left.

I just couldn't utter the words.

Fortune Cookies

I

We were scared, and it was dark;
the salt on our sweat tasted like water—
there seemed no light, even when it was day,
and we were falling face first on the concrete path to the
end of it all.

The lightning had just struck and burnt us,
and we were nothing but trembling carcasses
holding hands and losing grip;
slipping every time we took a step, undecided,
unknowing, reluctant to find each other.

We were shivering.
It was just about over,
and the end was inevitable
as our faith crumpled like burning paper
on which we had written our zombie vows
and promises of a whole love that was to

last decades *(supposedly)*.

But the fortune cookies were inedible,
and the Magic 8 Ball was telling us incomprehensible lies
as we still acted like phony know-it-alls,
unwilling to let go the last of what remained,
even when what remained was shaken, barren, and
amputated.

II

At times the future disappears
as the present throws up sickness onto the eyes of the
dreamers,
and often it is to scare us.

The immortal bonds are mortified
as they gasp for air,
and the steel-sharp strength in our heart rusts quicker
than we would have ever imagined
while making plans of where to spend the rest of our life.

These are times when our love is put to test.

And the love that fails those tests often dies the death of
a coward; sweating, crying, and begging to be allowed to
live.

No doubt such cowards are set free
by the weak hangmen
who don't know how to do their job well—
destined to be forever tracing bread crumbs
with their tails wagging
and their tongues dangling out of their greedy mouths,
spitting venom for glue,
to repair the earth-sized holes that exist in their hearts.

And these words echo every time a poor
soul takes them in for love:

"Cowards find love, but they don't know how to keep it."

Tragedy

The tragedy of love is in its ending,

the blessing—everything else.

No love ever deserves to end.

Your Soul Needs Caring Too

How strong have you been acting all this while. You have kept it together even when your world is shattering and your heart scattering into tiny pieces which hardly beat for anything anymore. And I know, you think you can keep going like this. I know, you think you are strong enough for the both of you. I know, you think it is your duty to heal them, and I know, you think things will change only if you hold on a little longer. You have been thinking like this for years now. And the reality is that nothing has changed. And you are not strong enough. At least not for the both of you for now. And actually, it is not your duty to hold them together anymore.

Some people become one only after they are thrown off the bridge, in pieces, like confetti, and that is how they feel free. You cannot keep their pieces clenched in your fist and think they are one.

Yes, they are broken. And so are you. You will heal once you open your fist and get your hand back. That same hand which was once meant to be held with love, by choice, and passionately. It doesn't matter how hard you hold your weakness, it will still remain a weakness, unless you let go. And if you want to know the true resilience in you—let go.

You have become used to having half of everything in

your life by now. Half a lover, half a love, half the attention, and that's how you have confused half for whole now. You have long forgotten that you deserve more. That you are whole. That you are enough. Enough to create life. Enough to start families. Enough to care for generations and most importantly, enough to be alone.

Yes, you are strong. But you are only strong for yourself for now. You don't know, because for years you hardly ever have looked inside of you to understand that your soul needs caring too. It needs to be pampered. And believe it or not, now is your time.

Falling Out of Love

"Love conquers everything, except the hearts of two people

falling out of it—tragedy of the utmost kind."

Lesson

We can't hold on to people in our lives who don't know the truth of us.

Dream

Tonight

I wrote

a dream;

Your kiss

and

my smile.

Wishes

I want the sane kiss,

    the slow dance,

    fingers tangled on our backs.

I want the sober nights,

    messed-up sheets,

    sloshed minds high on sweat.

I want the tired sleep,

    and you resting

    back on your side of the bed.

Swim

All your life, you have

drowned in my ocean.

Now you learn to swim.

Last Touch

I

Like raindrop on a rose petal
A diamond glittering in vain;
Love suffers in all its kindness
Withers under its own weight

Like sorrow in all whispers
Boundless hurt in every take;
We're trapped in glass frames
Those shine and then break.

From lunacy of lovers
To this levity of heartbreak;
Vanquished angels stand ready
In hurricanes of rage

Iron pipes of perfection
To rusty creeks of decay;
Revolts and rebellions—

All destined to fail

The last touch oh! So weary
The last kiss—so mundane
Good-byes are not demons;
Cremated angels remain.

II

Weaving and then unweaving
This facade with tender hands
Ready, steady, and silence;
About time for another plan.

The lonely meadows in our chests;
Places for demons to breathe.
Uncanny frenzy of lovers
They laugh and then they weep.

Finders keepers of gems
Losers weepers and sheep;
Wet smooches for paragons
Sour whiskey for creeps

Hope

I hope you are all right.

I hope the sea of joy is washing your feet.

I hope the kite you flew reached its moon of freedom

before you ran short of string

and finally you feel free.

I hope you found what you were looking for

without visiting deserts of futile lovers

to feel the warmth you so deserved

in every sip you take of this life.

I am not waiting for you, lover.

However, I am waiting for you to find your lost joy.

I am waiting for you to reach where you'd set out to

reach,

and I am rooting for you

as I pray;

reciting verses from battles

fought by brave warriors just so you win this fight.

I hope you win this fight.

And once you do, I hope you open your hands

and let go of the anger you carry in your fists.

Love awaits you.

But before you see it,

I hope the devil in your angel eyes finds peace.

Absolutes

On the run from something or someone,
always away from where I should be...
When will I reach the place,
the mirage of which I have been chasing for years now?

Maybe if I stop, breathe,
and hold my legs as anchors to the ground...
Maybe if I give up looking,
and take up feeling all that exists in my soul,

and maybe if I let this universe do its magic
and bring to me what it deems fit;

Maybe then,
what I have been looking for comes
and finds me.

And maybe I too find the absolutes in the midst of it all.

And maybe then, just maybe
this *maybe* goes away for good.

Heartache

Her taste doesn't leave my lips, but
the unspoken words are gagging my
conscience into another life away
from this—

With more lips to kiss, more hearts to
break, more ache to earn, more death to
live.

Fairies and Wolves

There are straight lines that circle under my skin, and
I am looking for a hand that can trace them in simpler
ways.
Complexities are derogatory excuses spat onto your
being
by the ones unwilling to feel the urge in you —

To be loved,

To be cared for,

And in rare instances — to be felt,

And the person who speaks to your heart is the one that
can truly speak to you.

But what speaks to you more than books written for
children about fairies and wolves?

. . . .

Who can be my fairy, when everyone seems to be the wolf?

And the question I am asking is, Who can love us as purely as the stories in those children's books?

Chaos

I don't think I will kiss you tonight.
I don't want to squander another night.

I think I will just hover around your eyes for a while
and see you drift into the lap of deep sleep.

It has been chaos in my head lately,
but now that I have met you,
I see how chaos can be beautiful too.

After all, it led me to you.

The Kind We Deserve

I am tired of watering the simple and

watching it grow into something so complex.

I want just the simple now,

I want the ordinary—untwisted and

without complication.

I want to nurture it and watch it slowly

blossom into something special; the kind we deserve.

The Worst Is Over

The universe on your skin is empty
from all the silence on your tongue.
Forgive yourself. Let your body heal
from all the wounds you did not inflict
on yourself. Drop the sword you carry
on your shoulder for self-defense.
Lower the armor you hold high up
for protection. Those who harmed you
are not going to come back. Those who
have left never intended to return.

You Are Complete

"You complete me," she said.

"Don't say it," I interrupted her mid-sentence.

"Don't say what?" she questioned, cross-eyed and puzzled.

"This! I am everything. I complete you nonsense. You are whole already. You were born full; absolutely complete. And then these stupid boys came along and made you feel like a fragment. Like you had to rely on others for the rest of your pieces. Like you always need someone to feel worthy. Like you are only someone when you are part of someone else's identity. Like lips are the only places you could be safe in. Like you would burst into flames if you didn't want to give yourself away. Like you were some second class citizen when you're lonely. Like you are useless if alone. Like the world wouldn't see you on your own. Like you're some kind of ghost wandering aimlessly unless someone takes your hand and guides you to the ways of humanity.

No. They were just boys, don't you see. They didn't know what they were doing. They were the ones who were lacking. After all they had a lot of growing up to do.

But you, you are a woman. And a woman lives inside every girl from the very beginning. From the time she is conceived.

You are complete, always remember that. You were always complete."

Simple

No poetic verve

No musical abstraction

Read this and understand:

You keep me warm.

Love Yourself

You are drowning in the effort it takes you to smile. It was not supposed to be this bad. They were going to end this lifelong pain. Look now. They didn't. Just like everyone who had come before them. Who had promised you the same things. The same dreams. The same future.

What will you do now? Will you love yourself the way you deserve to be loved, or will you betray yourself as well? Don't you know the years you have neglected your own self count too? Hasn't anybody told you what years of self-pity do to a person? Don't you understand all this hatred you secretly house for your own self and everyone else who left you alone is the worst form of self-abuse?

It is not only they who left you; you have done it to yourself a hundred times too. And the worst part of it all is that you don't even know it.

Please love yourself.

Hearts

Those convinced of their heart's ferocity have never had their world taken away from them, and those boasting of their heart's fragile nature have hardly ever witnessed a true tragedy in life.

I don't know from where this notion began. But hearts are not strong, and neither are they fragile. Hearts are rather persistent. They have learned the art of perseverance. They keep beating. They keep carrying on. Just like the kind of love affairs that never end.

Adam and Eve

We have shown this world the
meaning of compassion.
We have fought them, yet
adored them still.
We have spoken fiercely of all that was in us,
yet with patient ears we
have heard them.

I won't say that we have been
the Adam and Eve of earth.
We sure were not the first to
arrive on this land of
pretense and mistrust.
But I am sure as hell that in
some place away from this,
in some time different than this,
we have been the Adam and Eve of
love.

Hope*(less)*

Every morning

I wake to you

And

Every morning

I find you gone.

Forever.

Hope(*ful*)

To this place I came whole,
and in pieces I leave.
No glue was ever made in this world
to mend these earth-sized cracks
to make me whole again.

If you listen closely,
during the dead of night,
when everything else is silent,
you will hear oceans in my chest
that lie restless but still warm with hope.

I have this disease—hope.
Even when the lust for life seems fading,
I begin dreaming of an afterlife that is full
with sanctity of hope.

The day my body disintegrates from my soul,
my soul will not disintegrate from the idea of hope.

Maybe that is what will make me whole again.
Maybe hope is what makes us all whole.

I Think of You

When the night

comes to break my heart,

I think of you.

A Necessity

They warned me that only brave men could love a fierce woman like her, and in no way did I fit the description of the brave and the courageous. However, for me, loving her was never a choice but a necessity—like breathing; if I didn't do it, it would be the end of my life.

Like a Garden

With the claim of love, all expectations should end,
for love is not a remedy for the old aches you carry in
your bones,
rather something that makes you forget that you even
have bones.

Don't enter love with claims of infinite passion,
for the flame that burns too bright dies too soon as well.
Don't enter love with expectations to be loved back, for
you can fall in love a hundred times and not even once
be loved in return.
Don't enter love to give or ask favors,
for that will make it a transaction.

Enter it like you enter a garden,
and be prepared to be struck by hornets and cupids
alike.

Reason for My Being

From the moment your lips start extending

into your cheeks

to the moment that smile reaches your eyes,

reflecting through how you see me,

I hold my breath

and stop blinking.

So much so

that if one day I can't make you smile anymore,

I will be left with nothing but wandering sand in my

eyes

and impending death in my lungs.

When you are not smiling,

the only reason for my being is to make you.

Tinsel and Ornaments

How long will we pretend to be older than we are?

How more would we let the sober rule us?

How is it we don't see that we are traditions

of eggnog and cookies,

tinsel and ornaments.

We are Winter Wonderland by the fire;

cozy and young,

tipsy, festive,

deeply colored,

and forever madly in love.

In Hiding

I hear the winter breeze hymn your name in this foreign

land, see grass creep out of the crevices

of concrete pavements just so it can feel buried under

your bedazzling feet.

The pigeons stand ready,

holding letters that madmen have written to you,

And the saints beg demons for one single vision

of your gleaming skin.

Where are you, my love?

Are you in hiding, for you are saving yourself for me?

Or have you just turned your face the other way?

In Circles

(i)   Will it always be the pain? Will it always hurt?
      You trickle down my spine and chill my bones.

(ii) Dissolve the mystery and watch them disappear.
      Were we just playing mind games and calling it love?

(iii) How do I call my October magic as well?

(iv) Your voice rings true, and the deafening is clear.
      The music in my head plays well with silence.

(v)   Ruins of all that ruins me have made homes
      inside my blood.
      I keep building walls around myself.

(vi) Knock at the door. It is just the mailman.
      I surrender to my bed again.

(vii) There is laughter I hear.
      It can only come from the future.

(viii) I wish to fall into the arrival fallacy.
      I want to believe that good things will come.

(ix) Will you come?

Permission

She doesn't like the moon as I do
Says it borrows light from the sun
And she has been taught to ask for
permission.

At night when she kisses me good night
And in the morning when she hugs me good-bye
I think that is when she asks me for permission—
To enter my heart and borrow a little joy.

I don't tell her of my past;
About what I have done and where I come from.
Because I know
that all my life I have been borrowing without
permission—
Stealing kisses without pacts
Poaching affairs without a future.

And I fear she won't like it if she knows.

So I hold her like a baby

Get lost in her weary eyes

And hug her tight as we sleep

Maybe this is my way of asking permission

Maybe this is how I reform.

Love So Far

From one shattered heart to another
From a glass full to the ones peacefully broken;
A fountain tosses stream after stream
And the French wine keeps pouring firsthand
Straight onto the droughty tongue—
Quenching and replenishing thirst all at the same.

This is how it has been so far;
Kind and at times ruthless
Gentle and on occasion malevolent—
Like breeze on the day of storm.

Your Name

I sit here

in prostration,

Give me a name

to pray.

My sinful heart

wants to—

believe in

god again.

I Can Wait

If the kiss of another is what it takes

to wake you up again to the idea of love;

I will shed this skin,

I will peel my face,

I will break my very bones

and rebuild myself into something new.

You were born for this.

You have life waiting in your womb

and your whole being biding, to nurture it,

to bless it with the grace of your touch.

If you run from the idea of love,

let me run with you,

for maybe somewhere near the finish line

you feel loved again.

I can wait.

Disclaimer

I am one part courage
and three parts fear,

three parts love
and one part bitter;

half risen from rock bottom
and half still in free fall.

You can either love me whole
or not love me at all.

Wanderlust

Road our home, love in our hearts and wanderlust
billowing from our fingertips;
They will make a monument in our name and then
wonder which city to put it on.

Breathe

Wallow in pain, and one day you shall master it.

Till then, simply breathe and embrace this life,

For it is only you who can be you, and it is only

you who is brave enough to face each day anew.

Communication
(Saying I Love You)

Tell me happy when I tell you sad,

and I will tell you noble when you tell me flat.

You and I,

as we quietly daze out of distaste and frenzy into flavor,

away from routine and dipping into different.

We were made of stardust when this began,

and our memories are tokens to remind us

that we are still no less than able magic wands and shiny

crystals;

only if we say the magic words to feel the spell again.

How?

Years from now, if we get a chance to meet,

how will we look each other in the eyes

and not reminisce about what once was;

what once was and what will never be.

How will we greet our smiles

if they decide to peek out from our wrinkled faces

when you see me, and I you,

and how then will we go back to our glower and frown?

How will we sit across and not hold hands

after all these draining years,

and if we do,

how then will we stop?

How will we let go that time around?

From where will we find the courage?

Find Your Inner Beauty

You are so used to calamity that you feel ugly in the calm. Tragedy has been your normal for too long now. Every catastrophe has taken a little away from you, but believe it or not, the biggest misfortune of your life has always been you looking for your soul mate while neglecting your own soul.

Spring

Yes, she was lonely.
But someone had told her
That the flowers, the scents, the colors might wither
and fade away with time.

But if there is love,
there is compassion
If there is need to be,
to survive;

the roots will help the plant live on forever.
And no plant with the zeal to live
and the roots to back that zeal
can be stopped from spewing new flowers,
new fruits, new scents the next season.

Yes, she was lonely,
but in no way was she bitter,
for she knew naked and lonely in autumn
doesn't mean naked and lonely in the spring.

Confession

I see a forlorn little angel nest in your sunburst hair, and my eyes become invitations for you to come and rest on my quiet shoulder.

"I am a sad person generally, you know," I confess in a soft whisper.

"I figured," you reply, "that is why you are always smiling so much."

How We Fall In Love

There is a certain kind of beauty in the parts of yourself that you consider ugly. Your scars no matter how unsightly—will always hold a certain memory; a distinguished lesson. And I think after a certain age, you don't attract lovers as much as you attract certain special people who love to hover over your scars and examine the stories held in their crescents.

These people don't see you or your scars as beautiful or ugly, rather they transcend into your soul through these openings just to honor their own curious minds.

These people understand how pious a person is, with all their scars. They know what it takes to undergo pain and still be there, standing tall. And it is there and then, these marvelous, curious souls fall in love with all that they see, with all that they feel.

This is how love begins after a certain age. How can you not respect that? How can you not let them in?

Epidemic

So often we confuse mistakes for soul mates, lessons for lovers, and at the same time worthy life partners for one-night stands.

It's an epidemic.

Defences

The fact of the matter is that we become too comfortable being alone at times, or at least that is what we tell ourselves. Being alone is not bad, enjoying solitude in no way is a curse, but it is the proud feeling in it that is unbecoming; the recurring theme in our life if we don't take care, if we aren't cautious enough.

Yes, you cannot invite love into your life at will. But you have to let it in when the time is right and it graciously comes knocking at your door.

Question

What if

you are all

there is

and

somehow

I lose you?

Always

Even when

they erase

all my colors,

I will

still be

painted black

with the

memories of you.

Revolution

You want a revolution?
Start loving yourself.

For Yourself

There is only that much of ourselves we have that we can give, and often times there are undeserving people who take it all away. Beware of the thieves. Beware of the takers. They will leave you with years of having nothing to give to the ones who actually deserve your all.

Save some for yourself.

Wishes

Come see, the butterflies died.

The shadows of their carcasses are still there,

in me somewhere, and in you.

But it doesn't tickle anymore.

Come see, the smiles are no more.

Their fragments buried deep in my thoughts of you,

and in you, the thoughts of me.

They are guarding our wounds so they

don't hurt anymore.

Come see, the wishes closed their eyes.

They broke free, time and again,

only to be silenced by our demons.

Now they lie buried under the heavy

burden of our lies;

They don't cry. They don't wish anymore.

Temporary Places

With her touch I knew this smile could linger a little longer. Her arms around my head, my head on her chest, her heart beating in soothing tone, and that feeling safe in the most temporary place I could find.

This calm was the last of the comfort and what was to happen was weeks of heartache. The choice was obvious.

"Just a little longer," I whispered,

and just like the candle burning twice as bright before flickering to darkness, her grip around me tightened, and then she said my name.

Good-byes are so obvious at times. So cliché. Yet always so devastating, so heartbreaking.

My Pretty Illusion

The stars were on fire that night,

as the warmth of your skin extinguished into ice.

I saw you falling out of love with me,

and as we parted ways,

I gasped for air,

just to fill my lungs with your scent one last time.

We shared our bed that night,

but the two inches that separated us

were enough to give me the taste

of the hell that was about to break loose.

I thought I knew heartache dearly,

but the next day, which I spent in the shower

rubbing your scent out of my aching bones,

that is when it hit me:

Distance cannot always be measured in miles.

Just like the moon which seems at arm's length certain

nights;

it is mostly a pretty illusion, that's all.

You will always be my pretty illusion.
There is a space in my heart that is for you,
and no matter how many times I fall in and out of love,
that space will always be for you.

You

There burns a star in my memory
And I am always lonely with the thoughts
of bringing it to life.

Dream

In our dream we met

and I broke the silence

that had kept us distant.

Your fingers ran on my skin,

in my hair—like butterflies hovering

from one rose to another,

fulfilling their lust.

In my dream,

I accepted your whispers,

without apology,

without resentment,

until a nightmare came and woke us up.

Nothing More

Just a moment more. Only a minute longer. Stay. Sit here and hold me. Let my massacred heart settle in its own death. Let my breathing come to a halt. Let my eyes dam up their flooding. Let my feet stop their trembling. Let my hands pause their quiver. Wait till this sweat desiccates. This calamity has to end. It seems with the taking of a life. Stay till then with me wearing a kind smile. Let me be reborn again. Into the time when I know not of you and you know not of me. And then let us meet again. But this time as perfect strangers. Where we have nothing to say to each-other but hello. Hello and nothing more.

Poetry

I have seen love turn into volcanoes so violent,

my heart is ash now.

It is ash now,

but the embers of memories in it still

burn like it was yesterday,

for yesterday is all I have;

you see, tomorrow somehow forgot

the way to my home.

Now is your time.

If you want to kill me, kill me now;

I want poets to write poetry on my death.

Just a Phone Call Away

Just a phone call away...
Call whenever you miss me.

Just a phone call away...
Often said like a medicine, as if your lover sitting next
to you while you sleep in your bed to the sound of their
breathing.

Just a phone call away...
The longest distance between two people when their
hearts stop belonging and their earths careen in different
ways.

Just a phone call away...
Like telephone companies having laid out thousands of
miles of wire throughout the land and underneath the
sea, mocking you in the face.

Just a phone call away...
Or (maybe) away for good.

Braces and Bruises

Amazing how everything shines in the morning light
when you see it with me,
and how even the aurora shies away
when you are gone.

That whelk on your cheek, you say
reminds you of your teenage years,
but what I see in it is a gift from god
to keep evil at bay.

You are like a hawk circling its kill,
with eyes as sharp as the thorns in roses
I keep giving you,
and then relentlessly you aim
straight at the apex of my heart.

What are you looking for, lover?
Someone to love?
Or someone to avenge all the missed love

in your teenage years of braces and bullies

and bruises and acne?

Because I am just your average Joe, lover;

the more you starve me of love,

the more I would want it.

Perplexity

My hands lie buried in your petal flesh

When there sleeps a winter in my autumn bones.

Dear Ones

Some names build dreams
inside us, and some break
our very bones.

Footsteps

Flowers sprout from under your feet

when you allow the soil to touch them,

and those very flowers burn hot red—petrified and jealous

every time you walk away.

Every footstep in the endless trail of footsteps

that you have left on this earth,

from everywhere you have been,

remains in battle to this day,

for each one of them fights with the next

to have the honor of being buried

under your feet again.

Our Story

Ours was not the saddest story.

Some people don't even get to taste love.

Self-Doubt III

At times, I wish I had the pomp and the frills it takes to survive when the mirror starts lying to my face. But more often than not, all I can do is stand my ground stripped of my veneer, clenching desperately on to the truth lying barren in the palm of my hand, that *I am enough.*

Because I have come to understand that if we say we are enough, enough times, the mirror will know that we have finally called its bluff.

Always

There is a part of me that
will always belong to you
and in that part of me, I
will always hurt.

Marvelous Misfit

You were the solitary reaper with mystic eyes,

lending hands to plough fields that didn't belong to you,

and hence your harvest was always meager;

much less than you deserved.

I was the whistling wind,

going through the weeping willow tree,

rattling what life it bore;

stealing the last of the water that floated its leaves.

You were the welcome sign,

I was the escape plan,

And we were never a match;

always a marvelous misfit.

Realization

It is only when you watch them walk away

that you realize how much you truly

wanted them to stay.

Love is tricky like that.

It sneaks up on you at the point of no return,

revealing its true form only at the very end.

and god, does it hurt when it introduces

itself like that.

Lullabies Unfit for Kids

I create elastic lovers out of suitors
and I push them to test the recoil.
Many never come back.
Many break with my tests,
and I,
I die a little every time
I hear the noise of someone's heart breaking
because of me.
And my heart always plays harmonies with that sound;
every time an octave higher than the last.

If you counted the pieces that beat inside my chest,
you would fall asleep counting the failed potential in
each.
You see, the broken pieces of my heart sing lullabies—
the ones unfit for kids.
It is crazy inside where my heart lives.

How stupid of it,
to still be singing sleeping pills out in my name.
I wonder, when it stops beating,
will I finally wake up or fall asleep for good?

Murder

She exhaled gently onto me,

like when one blows over tea to cool it down

before taking the first sip.

But I was in ruins already.

Completely and utterly burned from last time.

I was cold ash before she had even arrived,

and when her breath hit me,

even though so tender,

I vanished into thin air,

and once again she lost me.

(And we thought we would find no excuse to let go this time.)

Going back to an old lover can be suicide, they told me.

It is murder, I replied.

Once upon a Time

Once upon a time not long ago, I built a fire in you. Now I hope you find someone who doesn't let that fire go to waste.

True Love

We are often too scared to fall out of a love that was never there, and generally the love we find is nothing but our own fear of being alone.

True love is rare, and the possibility that we might have never had it makes us believe that we had it even more.

Majestic View

There is rhythm to silence just like there is color to night, and as I paint your skin with gentle strokes, the evening gets to pause its own silence and dip in our tunes.

"The moon shines brighter than usual tonight?" you break our kiss and ask.

"It has to enjoy the majestic view, after all," I reply.

At the End of It All

We are lovers and we are fighters; *pencils and sharpeners*
We are grownups and we are children; *oil paints and
crayons*
We are acrylics and we are papers; *creators and shredders*

Learning the art of love from the destruction of self,
Immersed in paintings of different phases of the moon:

that are sharp and that are round,
that are silver and that are brown,
that are buoyant and that have drowned,
that are free and that are bound,

and we know nothing but this:

to give of ourselves a little
until we give of ourselves more,
and it doesn't matter if nothing
remains of us at the end of it all.

Red Lips

She is red marks on the neck
     in sleepless nights;
     wet kisses, red lips
     and endless smiles.

She is tummy ache gotten
     from excess laughing;
     a breathless pause
     during happy talking.

She is delight you dream
     with eyes open;
     ogling a face
     and never stopping.

Memories

Go away, the memories,

for today I have things to do.

Beauty

Beauty often slows me to a halt;

stunned with wonder.

When I sit in long flights across continents,

and the thought of death creeps into my mind,

I start looking anxiously for it;

a kind smile, a toddler's squeal,

a motherly face, a gentle soul,

And my thoughts instantly change from death,

to the possibility of death with a smile.

Growing up

Her tears always—

the voice of the girl

dying inside.

The Feeling May Remain

The orange of the light and the gray of the dark
have already parted,
the anguish of separation and the smiles of union
reached their abysmal end.

Yet
the burning in the heart,
the sour on the tongue,
and the bitterness of the young
have not left.

The nights of suffering still hold their weight.
The metaphors of longing still remain true.

For whatever you know, know this about love:

even when all is said and done,
when you have moved on and
all the strings in reach have been strung,

there will still live a storm in you—hard to decimate—
and for a while, and always, that feeling may remain.

Midnight

She changed,

and I witnessed it with bloodied eyes

and a sense of wonderment and regret.

She was the blossom in the sun,

but now it was midnight's turn to tend to her needs.

All her life she had given all like she was taught to.

Now it was her turn to take it all back.

And I swear the sun set early on days

she craved the dark,

and she stood there unruffled—dancing to the silence

of her night and the calamities to come.

Hurricane and a Rainbow

She was the kind of girl you know you don't want to go near.

There was chaos in her sadness,

Yet her smile had healing power of the prophets.

She was a hurricane and a rainbow packed in one.

Equals

We were both equals;

A chapter in each other's life.

Ghosts

There is a fragrance chafing at me from one corner of the room; Lavender oil sticks liberating scents of dead flowers, killing me in little bouts of melancholy, from the time we bought them at the West Side store. One photo frame stares at me from the other end, as if trying to talk me into calling you.

Our favorite memories become more vivid as time passes. Some scientists now say that we remember them the way we want to and not how they actually happened at the time. I would believe those scientists, if only I didn't feel your ghost sitting next to me every night, telling me all these tales from our glorious past.

Ghosts are weird beings. Contrary to popular belief, they don't tell you much about the future. Maybe that is why some lovesick scientist in some Ivy League school's neuropsychology lab deemed them to be the creations of our own minds. I, on the other hand, deem them to be manifestations of love stories cut short by circumstance.

More

Believe in kissing

Let it mean something

more.

In Pieces

Your eyes smell like them,

and I am ready to lick the salt off your cheeks.

Your skin wringing oceans of their names,

and your soul stained only with their memories.

I see the sun in you.

I feel the warmth you don't feel.

All I want is a little piece of your heart

to fall in love with the (w)hole I have

beating inside my ribcage for you.

*(I don't know if you know, but sometimes, hearts have to love
in pieces too.)*

Poem

How do I translate all that I assemble

in my desperate attempt from the vast oceans of your

life,

into something so routine as black and white?

No, I can't contain you in a poem;

I am sorry.

All I can do is try.

Tattoos

Tattoos are nothing but scars, but what better way to honor something than keeping it permanently engraved on our skin?

I have no tattoo for anyone to see, but the fact of the matter is, scars that are flesh deep cannot be seen anyway.

Promise

I will meet you far from sorrow
and away from this hustle of life.

I will meet you in the middle of
a love song.

Masks

How I am flooded with all of you,

but drowning is not an option.

So I love you from a distance,

for distance is my shield.

I miss you in the dark,

for the dark hides my face.

I touch you in my dreams,

for dreams have to end.

My heart breaks, but my suffering —

I don't let it spill.

My eyes water, but my tears —

I don't let them flow.

My hands tremble, but my weakness —

I don't let it show.

So here we are now,

together, and so alone.

Self-Doubt IV

Then I saw her.

Her skin, her face, her freckles,

her eyebrows, and finally her words.

And I thought to myself,

How remarkably she portrays herself;

so free,

so spirited,

so perfect.

And yet how consciously flawed

she would be to herself.

Although, to her, there was more;

she looked even more beautiful wearing her flaws.

Unfortunately,

she was blind to her own beauty, as are we all.

Blue

In me, there are oceans of you.

Through my eyes, they can see the blue.

Tomorrow

In my life good-nights have meant good-byes.

So, let us not say a word.

Just kiss and walk our separate ways

in hope that maybe tomorrow

we find each other again.

Soon

There is an earthquake fast asleep in my bones,

and my hands shake in fear of the revolution to come.

You don't erase a name from your memory

and not change in massive form.

The body has to shiver before it settles into its calm

again.

The blood has to freeze before it touches new warmth

again.

Die. Wilt. Wither in anticipation.

The spring will be here soon.

Fortune Teller

"Poison! Poison!" screams the fortune teller.
"You are dating all the wrong types. There are demons roaring on your shoulders, hindering your growth.

"Bitter! Bitter!
"There is so much sugar in your blood, in your eyes, and not enough on your tongue. Drink your tears. Pour blood into your song.

"Teacher, teacher.
"There is no need for you to pop pills. No purpose for defibrillator pads or guns or companions or anything you think you need for survival. You need a guru to teach you how to breathe, a dervish to show you how to think straight.

"Poem, poem.
"You have way too many lines in the palms of your hands; too many lines and too little fortune. All there is in there is pain. All there is in there is poetry. There are sonnets seeping into your veins. There are ghazals sprouting on the back of your hands."

"Everything I let go turns into free verse. Everything I

let slip away takes form of these words. I am not one to hold the future up for ransom. Fortune has no place in the palm of my hands. Lovers cannot be prisoners—and this is not a war.

"And, dear fortune teller, I don't regret the clouds that get in my way. I don't question the pace of my life or all the hindrance. Everybody that I have come across, everything that I have done, all that I have gone through, and all that I have endured has shaped me to be the person that I am today. And no one can take this away from me. Don't you know we need all of everything to be the person we become?"

Shallow and Deep

You have rehearsed long enough in shallow waters to finally tread safely in the deep end. Even though you have heard countless stories of people drowning, understand, life spent in denial is not a life at all.

It is about time you swim into the depths and give at least one good story to the fear you have been calling love for so long.

Self-Love

You are heartbroken, and then someone comes along and breaks you even more. Especially when you expect them to be your savior. And it happens again and again. You get into this rut of lovers who don't know what to do with you. You start to shrink back into yourself. Begin to take cover in your own skin. You start digging holes in people and calling them shelters. Your self-esteem is gone. So is your confidence. You start to think it is all your fault. Like it is you who doesn't deserve any better.

Then one day you wake up, and no one is there but your own thoughts. For the first time in years, you are completely alone. And you realize the beauty of solitude. Days turn into weeks, and weeks into months. And then it hits you:
You have been dumbing yourself down for the sake of others to feel good. Moulding yourself into people you were not just to fit in their expectations of you. And doing this, you'd lost respect for yourself. And when you lose respect for yourself, there can be no one who respects you. And now when you know solitude, you understand, there is one person who has to love you first for others to love you too. It is the person looking back at you when you stand in front of the mirror every morning before you leave the house.

Self-love is the form of love that leads to everything else. It comes first, and then come all other forms of love. And now you know it. And now you are ready for it.

Firsts

Let me tell you something about your first love. The bitter truth is that it will end. It will inevitably rip you apart into so many pieces, no matter how hard you try, you will never get all of them back. It will wrench you of all the pretty tales you have heard of love, and you will feel like nothing but a fool. But if you survive all of that and look back on the times when you truly felt loved, you will understand that in between all the games, all the toxic tantrums, all the deceit, there were moments of pure magic. There were days when all your sanity was not in spite of but only because of love. You woke up many a morning only because it was there to push you out of bed and pull you into its allure. That alone will make you never give up on the idea of love. That is, of course, if you survive your first heartbreak.

The Year of Perspective

This year I learned of pain,
of reaching out to people
and learning to say I am not okay.

This year I taught that
brokenness is as common as casualty,
as beautiful as kindness.

This year I killed myself to be light,
gave up a lot, and gained a lot more.
Taught strangers to pronounce
my name right.

This year was for love and for solitude,
for smiling with people on the bus.

This year was for learning,
for knowing,
for understanding my body and my mind.

This year my name and my soul were one.

This year was for taking control,
for letting go.
for getting clarity into my thoughts,
for making friends with the confusion,
for making amends with my heart.

This year was for perspective,
a sense of looking at things in a new light.

And I say good-bye to this year with
immense gratitude, grace,
and a warm smile on my face.

About the Author

Akif Kichloo is a poet, doctor, musician, photographer, and artist of Indian origin who lives in New York City, New York with his awesome brother and adorable nephew Adam. A graduate of JU, Akif holds a bachelor's degree in medicine and surgery.

When he is not writing, clicking pictures or playing music, he is either busy looking after his patients or doing clinical research work in the field of anesthesiology.

Akif Kichloo started writing at an early age, having contributed for publications like The Huffington Post and The Wire, he continues to write for various newspapers and magazines internationally. In addition, he was invited to speak at the prestigious TEDx stage at Christ University to present his talk *Follow Your Confusion.*

Amidst the uncertainties of this amazing, magical, horrible, beautiful life, as he puts it, Akif Kichloo writes of love, grief, healing and self care, posting a couple of poems weekly to his various social media pages with a huge following of avid readers and poetry lovers from all over the world.

akifkichloo.com
akifkichloobooks.com
Instagram: @akifkichloo
Twitter: @akifkichloo
Facebook: facebook.com/akifkichloo
Pinterest: pinterest.com/akifkichloo
Tumblr: akifkichloo.com